What's in the Sky?

by Michael Teitelbaum

Table of Contents

Introduction

What do you see when you look up at the night sky? What are those bright lights? How far away are they?

The biggest and brightest light in the night sky is the moon. The small twinkling lights are stars. Sometimes we can see planets in the night sky too.

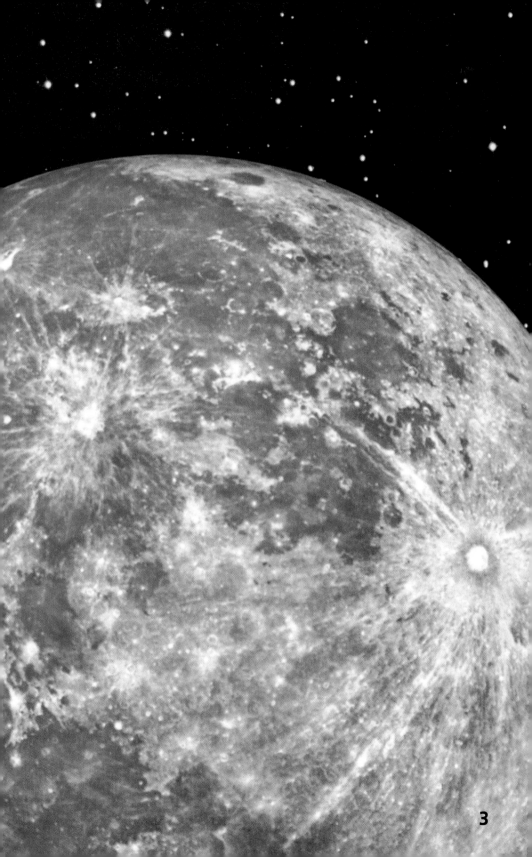

CHAPTER 1 The Moon

The moon is our nearest neighbor in space. It **orbits** around Earth. Not all planets have a moon. Some have more than one moon. Earth has only one moon.

What do we know about the moon? The moon is 239,000 miles (384,633 km) from Earth. We also know that the moon is a ball of gray rock and dust. And we know that the temperature on the moon can change from very hot to very cold.

Bigger or Smaller

From Earth the moon looks much bigger than the nearest planet, Venus. Distance is responsible. The moon is much closer to Earth. Venus is really almost four times larger than the moon. Venus is 26 million miles (41,842,944 km) from Earth.

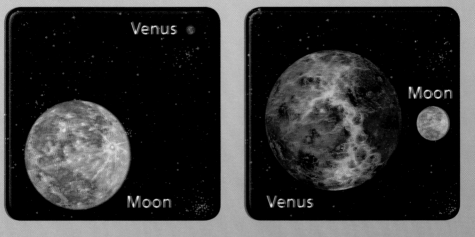

How It Looks From Earth   **Actual Size Difference**

Huge holes called craters cover the moon. They formed when large chunks of rock from space hit the moon. **Astronauts** who landed on the moon brought back moon rocks. Some of these rocks were more than one billion years old. How do we make that decision? Specialists take measurements. They use the measurements to tell how old rocks are. They communicate the facts.

Fast Fact

The "changes" that seem to take place as the moon goes around Earth are called phases.

Did You Know . . .

As the moon moves around Earth, it appears as a crescent, then as a half moon, and then as a full moon. Then it appears as a half moon, then back to crescent again. The entire trip takes about a month.

crescent moon

The moon does not make its own light. The moon is like a giant mirror. It reflects light from the sun and sends it to Earth.

Earth is a mirror too. It also reflects some sunlight that falls on it.

↻ This is an almost full moon rising over a city.

| half moon | full moon | half moon | crescent moon |

Stars

A star looks like a tiny point of light. But a star is really a giant ball of hot gas.

The sun is our closest star. That's why it looks bigger than other stars. On a clear night, you can easily see thousands of stars. Some stars look very bright. Others look dim. The stars that are very far away from Earth are the hardest to see.

Fast Fact

Stars are always in the sky. During the day the sky is too bright for you to see them.

Astronomers study the stars to find out what they are made of and how they create light. One of their essential jobs is to compare brightness of stars.

Groups of stars form pictures in the sky called constellations. The Big Dipper and the Great Bear are parts of constellations.

The Big Dipper

The Great Bear

Planets

Earth is a planet. It **revolves**, or travels, around the sun. But the seven other planets also orbit the sun. Together, these eight planets make up our solar system.

↻ There are eight planets in our solar system. This picture shows the order of the planets from the nearest to the farthest from the sun.

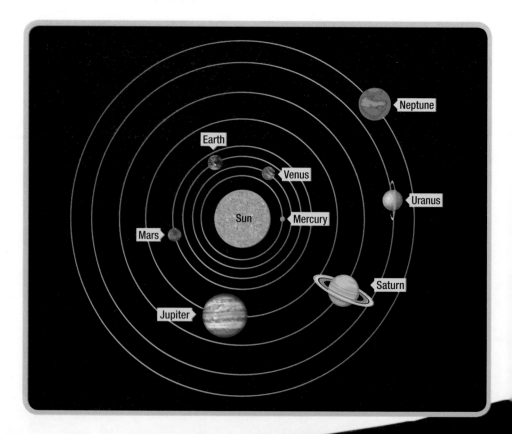

At times, you can see some planets in the night sky. Two planets are closer to the sun than Earth, and the others are all farther away.

Some planets are made of rock. Some planets have rings of ice, and some have more than one moon.

Did You Know . . .

People use powerful telescopes to research the night sky. The telescope makes things far away look close.

 The Milky Way

A very large group of planets and stars is called a **galaxy**. Earth's solar system is in the Milky Way galaxy. You can see the Milky Way on a very clear night with special glasses. It looks like a cloudy band running across the night sky.

◑ The Milky Way

The Milky Way is 100,000 light-years wide. A light-year is the distance you would travel if you moved at the speed of light for one whole year! Light travels 186,000 miles (299,338 km) each second!

In the Solar System		
	Asteroids	Big chunks of rock that go around the sun. Some are as big as a house.
	Comets	Big balls of ice, gas, and dust. The tail of a comet may be millions of miles long.
	Meteoroids	Bits of rock and metal. They are as small as grains of sand.

Conclusion

Tonight, when you look up at the night sky, you will probably see some wonderful sights. How will the moon look? What stars will you see? Will you see the Milky Way?

Glossary

astronaut *(AS-truh-nawt)* a person trained to fly in a spacecraft *(page 6)*

astronomer *(uh-STRON-uh-muhr)* a person who studies the stars and the planets *(page 9)*

galaxy *(GA-luhk-see)* a large system of planets and stars; for example, the Milky Way *(page 12)*

orbit *(AWR-bit)* to move in a path around another object *(page 4)*

revolve *(ri-VAHLV)* to go around something *(page 10)*

Index

Comprehension Check

Summarize

Use a chart to record events from the book. Then use the chart to summarize what you learned.

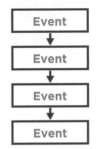

Think and Compare

1. Reread Did You Know on page 6. How does the appearance of the moon change? Write down the events. *(Sequence)*

2. Many stars have names. Would you like to have a star named after you? Why? *(Synthesize)*

3. Why do astronomers study the night sky? *(Evaluate)*